JAWS!

THE BIGGEST BITE!

SHARKS FOR KIDS

(Fun Facts & Trivia)

Children's Marine Life Books

Speedy Publishing LLC

40 E. Main St. #1156

Newark, DE 19711

www.speedypublishing.com

Copyright 2017

In this book, we're going to talk about sharks. So, let's get right to it!

WHALE SHARK

FUN FACTS ABOUT SHARKS

Unlike whales and dolphins that are mammals, sharks are fish. In fact, the whale shark is the biggest fish in the ocean. Here are some other fun facts about sharks.

SHARKS DON'T HAVE BONES

Sharks don't have any bones inside their bodies. Neither do their "cousins" rays and skates, which more than likely evolved from sharks millions of years ago.

nstead of bones, they have cartilage, similar to the cartilage in our noses. It's very strong, but less dense than bones and much more flexible.

PREHISTORIC SHARKS

SHARKS SWAM ON EARTH BEFORE DINOSAURS WALKED ON LAND

The first evidence of sharks on Earth dates back to 400 million years before the present day. That is a whopping 200 million years prior to the time that any dinosaurs walked on Earth. Surprisingly, sharks haven't changed much from their ancient ancestors.

MOST SHARKS ARE HARMLESS TO MAN

There are over 400 different species of sharks in waterways around the world. New species are still being found. There are only 30 species that will attack humans if they are threatened.

HAMMERHEAD SHARK

The Great White shark, the Bull shark, the Tiger shark, the Mako shark, and the Hammerhead shark have attacked human beings.

More people die each year from accidents with deer on the roads than sharks in the water.

GRAY REEF SHARK

It's been estimated that over 100 million sharks are killed by human beings every year. The average number of shark attacks on people yearly is only about 70 worldwide. Sharks don't really like the taste of people. Scientists believe that they attack people because they are mistaken for seals, a favorite food of sharks.

Sharks have a special sensing organ that people don't have called the Ampullae of Lorenzini. They are small jelly-filled pores that they use to pick up the tiny electrical signals that all living animals give off when they move or breathe.

Hammerhead sharks have very sensitive Ampullae of Lorenzini.

MOST SHARKS HAVE TO KEEP MOVING TO STAY ALIVE

Fish pump water over their gills, but most types of sharks can't do this. They have to push through the water by swimming to get the water to flow through their mouths as well as over their five to seven pairs of gills.

This means that most sharks have to keep swimming at all times in order to stay alive. Two notable exceptions are the nurse shark and the angel shark.

The nurse shark opens and then closes its mouth in order to move water over its sets of gills and the angel shark has a spiracle, which is a hole located behind its eye, for this purpose.

MEGAMOUTH SHARK IN WASHINGTON MARITIME MUSEUM

THERE AREN'T MEGA-SIGHTINGS OF THE MEGAMOUTH SHARK

Perhaps the world's strangest shark is the Megamouth shark. Scientists didn't know it existed until 1976. Its body can get to a length of about 16 feet, but its enormous mouth is about 3 feet in width. This strange shark has only been documented and witnessed about a dozen times.

For some unknown reason, sharks very rarely get cancer. Scientists are studying their cartilage and other body tissues to look for a cure for human cancers.

CARIBBEAN REEF SHARK

SOME SHARKS CAN PUSH THEIR STOMACHS THROUGH THEIR MOUTHS

Many types of sharks can eat almost anything, but once in a while they come across something that they can't digest, such as a tin can or the shell of a sea turtle. To get rid of the offending object, they can thrust their stomachs out through their mouths and spit it out.

SOMETIMES SHARKS LUNGE AT METAL OBJECTS

For some reason, sharks sometimes lunge at or attack objects made of metal. Scientists believe that the metal emits weak amounts of electricity, which confuses the sharks into thinking the object is alive and edible.

It's been shown that some fish species dream, but so far there's no scientific evidence that sharks dream.

Since most of them don't stop moving, they don't sleep in the same way that humans do. Their brains do go into cycles of rest, but the shark still keeps moving.

DERMAL DENTICLES OF A LEMON SHARK VIEWED
THROUGH A SCANNING ELECTRON MICROSCOPE

FACT 12
SHARKS DON'T HAVE SCALES LIKE FISH DO

Unlike fish, sharks don't have any scales on their outer surfaces. Instead, they have denticles, which are more like teeth than scales. As the shark grows to a larger size, its denticles fall off naturally, making way for new ones.

Most sharks have about 40 very sharp teeth in their mouths. Behind their front teeth they have as many as seven rows of teeth. If they get their teeth into something and a tooth breaks off, within a day or so, one of the replacement teeth moves into position in the front.

The subsequent rows of teeth are always larger than the teeth that were replaced so as a shark gets older, its mouth gets scarier and scarier.

It's not unusual for a shark to go through as many as 30,000 teeth throughout its life.

THE LARGEST SHARK TOOTH EVER FOUND WAS ABOUT 6 INCHES LONG

The Carcharodon Megalodon, which means "rough tooth, huge tooth," was a massive ancient shark that scientists believe is now extinct. Fossil teeth from this enormous sea monster have been found and they measure 6 inches in length.

This giant creature was so big that it was the same length as a Tyrannosaurus rex. Its jaws were so gigantic that it would have been able to consume a car.

Some people believe that a species of Megalodon might still be alive deep within the ocean depths. Other very large sea creatures have been found in modern times, so it's possible.

THE GREAT WHITE SHARK IS KNOWN AS WHITE DEATH

The Great White shark is the largest known fish that is an apex predator. Called the White Death because of its reputation as a killing "machine," a Great White shark can get as large as 30 feet in length. Its jaw has about 2/3 of the strength of the extinct T-rex dinosaur.

GREAT WHITE SHARK

It has a reputation as a maneater, which is partially true since 30–50% of all shark attacks on humans are due to Great Whites.

It's the only type of fish that checks out what's at the water's surface by lifting its head completely out of the water.

SHARK FINS ARE CONSIDERED TO BE A GOURMET DELICACY

In many parts of Asia, shark fins are considered to be a gourmet delicacy and they are used to create shark fin soup. Fishermen sometimes take the shark's fins off while it is still alive and throw it back into the water where it soon dies a cruel and painful death since it can't swim or breathe.

SHARK FIN SOUP, CHINESE CUISINE

GOBLIN SHARK

First seen off the coast of Japan in 1898, this strange shark is a very bizarre looking creature. It has a long snout with Ampullae of Lorenzini. It has beady eyes and its skin is a pinkish-gray color and it has flabby, soft muscles. The goblin shark is so monstrous looking that it's been given the nickname "Frankenshark."

The most scary aspect of this rather small shark is its jaws. It swims along the ocean floor detecting the electrical impulses of potential prey.

When it finds what it wants to eat, it juts its jaws completely out of its head and grabs its prey within its sharp teeth so it can swallow it whole.

FACT 18
SHARKS HAVE AMAZING SENSES

In addition to their ability to sense electrical impulses, sharks have other keen senses as well. They can hear potential prey in the water from a distance as far as 3,000 feet away.

They are best at hearing sounds that are low-frequency unlike the high-frequency sounds that dolphins use to communicate.

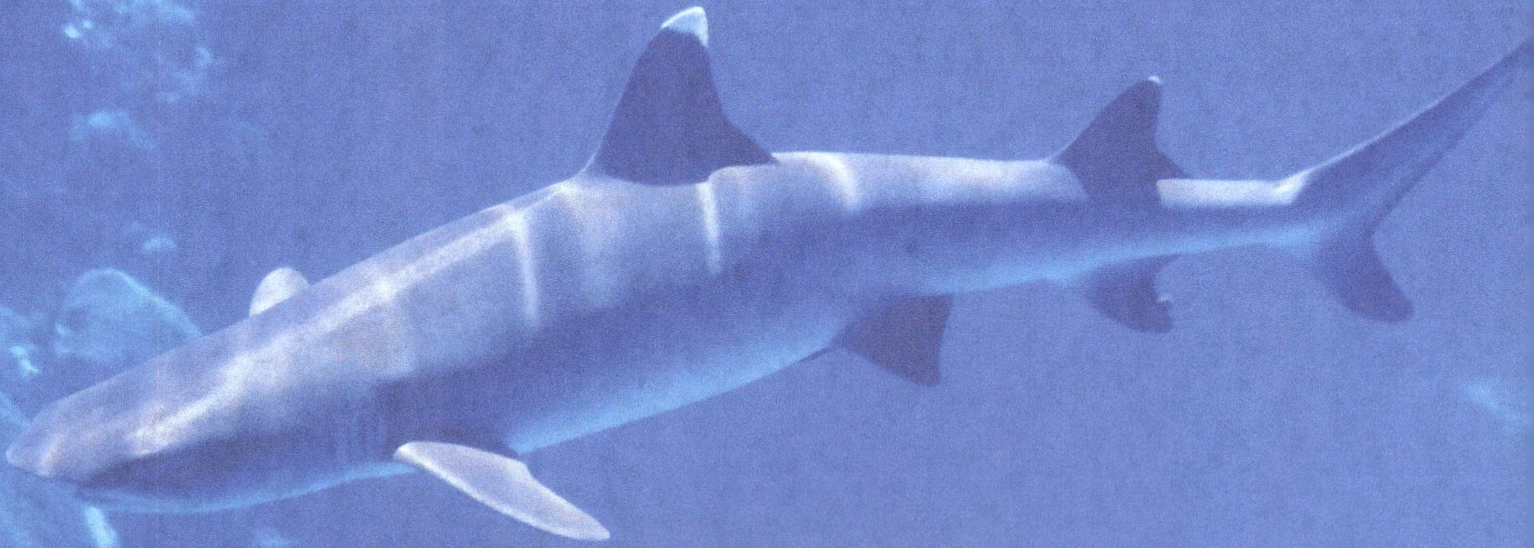

WHITETIP REEF SHARK

They can also smell a very small amount of blood or spilled guts in 100 million parts of water and can even detect the direction of the smell.

SHARKS SOLD IN THE PUBLIC MARKETS

SUMMARY

Most people are very scared of sharks, but the reality is that there are very few shark attacks worldwide. People are much more dangerous to sharks than the other way around. In fact, so many sharks are being killed that laws are being passed to protect them.

These fascinating fish are important to the food chains in all of the oceans so it's vital that they don't become extinct. They have lived on the Earth for about 400 million years.

TIGER SHARK

Awesome! Now that you've read about sharp–toothed sharks you may want to read about another animal with sharp teeth in the Baby Professor book Dinosaur Facts for Kids - Animal Book for Kids | Children's Animal Books.

Visit

BABY PROFESSOR
EDUCATION KIDS

www.BabyProfessorBooks.com

to download Free Baby Professor eBooks
and view our catalog of new and exciting
Children's Books